A DORLING KINDERSLEY BOOK

Editor Stella Love
Designer Karen Fielding
Managing Editor Jane Yorke
Production Jayne Wood

Photography by Dave King
Additional photography by Frank Greenaway (pages 8-9) and Jerry Young (pages 10-11, 16-17)
Illustrations by Jane Cradock-Watson and Dave Hopkins
Natural History Consultant Steve Parker
Animals supplied by Trevor Smith's Animal World, London Butterfly House, and Duisburg Zoo, Germany

Eye Openers ®
First published in Great Britain in 1992
by Dorling Kindersley Limited,
9 Henrietta Street, London WC2E 8PS
Reprinted 1993, 1994, 1996 (twice)

A CIP catalogue record for this book is available from the British Library.

ISBN 0-86318-872-9

Reproduced by Colourscan, Singapore
Printed and bound in Italy by L.E.G.O., Vicenza

·EYE·OPENERS·

Night-time Animals

Written by Angela Royston

DK
DORLING KINDERSLEY
London • New York • Stuttgart

Bushbaby

This little bushbaby wakes up at night. It climbs and leaps through the branches of jungle trees. A bushbaby uses its big ears and eyes to hunt for insects. It catches insects with its hands as they fly by.

ear
tail
hand

Bat

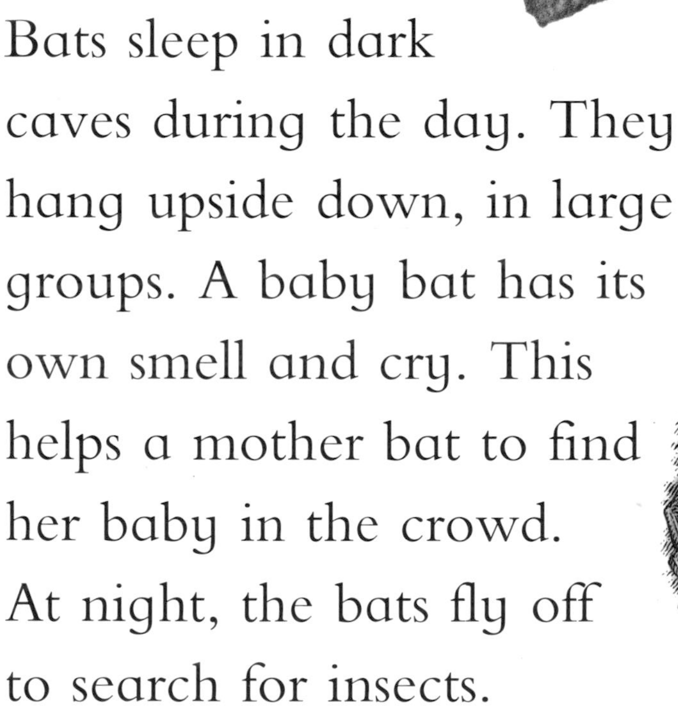

Bats sleep in dark caves during the day. They hang upside down, in large groups. A baby bat has its own smell and cry. This helps a mother bat to find her baby in the crowd. At night, the bats fly off to search for insects.

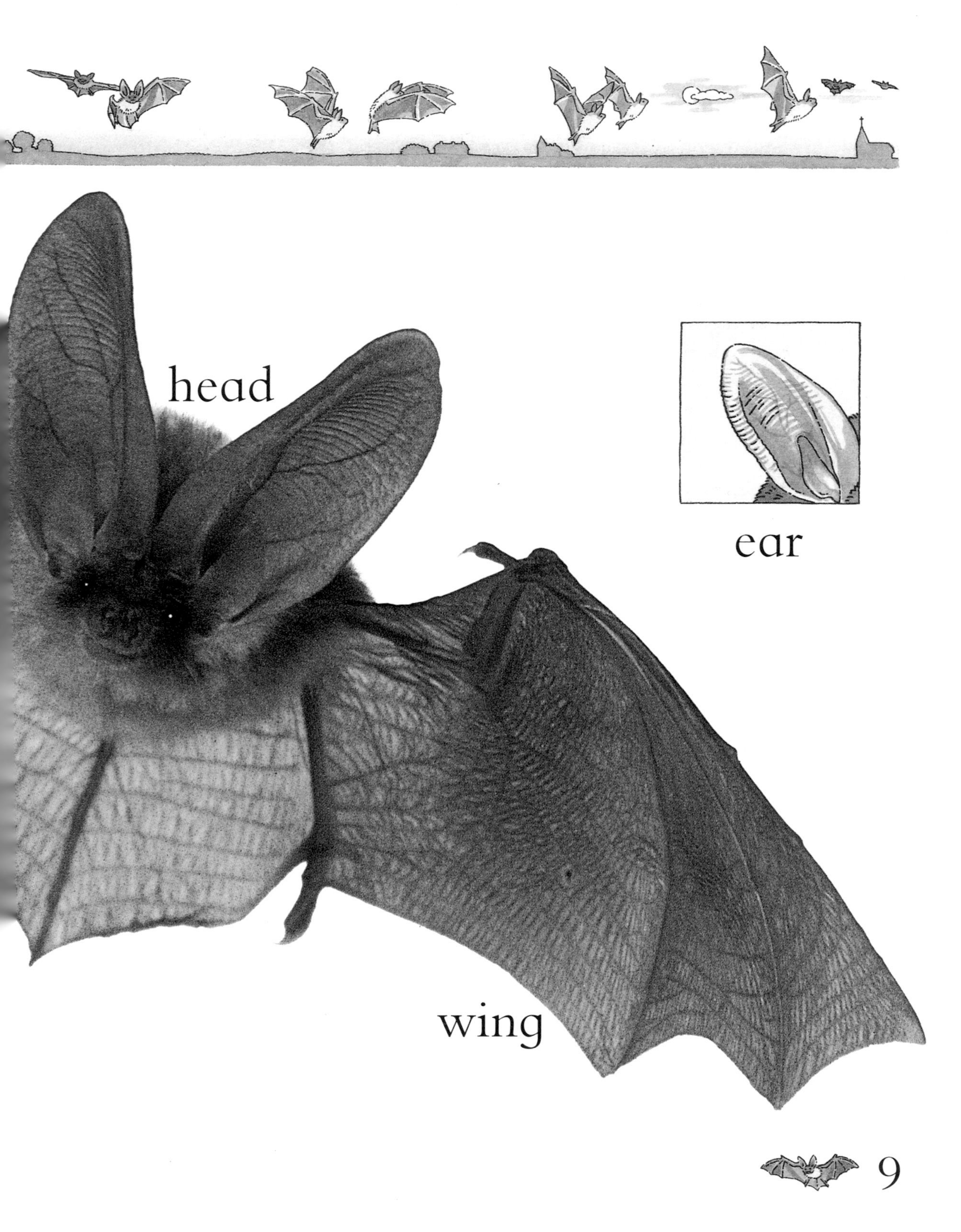
head
ear
wing

Fox

ear

These small foxes live in hot deserts. They spend the day sleeping in cool dens under the sand. At night, they come out to hunt for lizards and insects. The foxes hide from their enemies by burying themselves in the sand.

nose
paw

Owl

Some owls live in
old farm buildings.
At night, they fly low
over the ground hunting
for food. The owl's soft
wing feathers help it
to fly silently. It can
swoop down and catch
a mouse in its talons,
without making a sound.

head
feathers
tail
talons

Fieldmouse

Fieldmice nest in burrows underground. When it is dark, they come out to collect seeds, nuts, and berries. Fieldmice are good climbers, and can run fast. This helps them to escape from owls and other enemies.

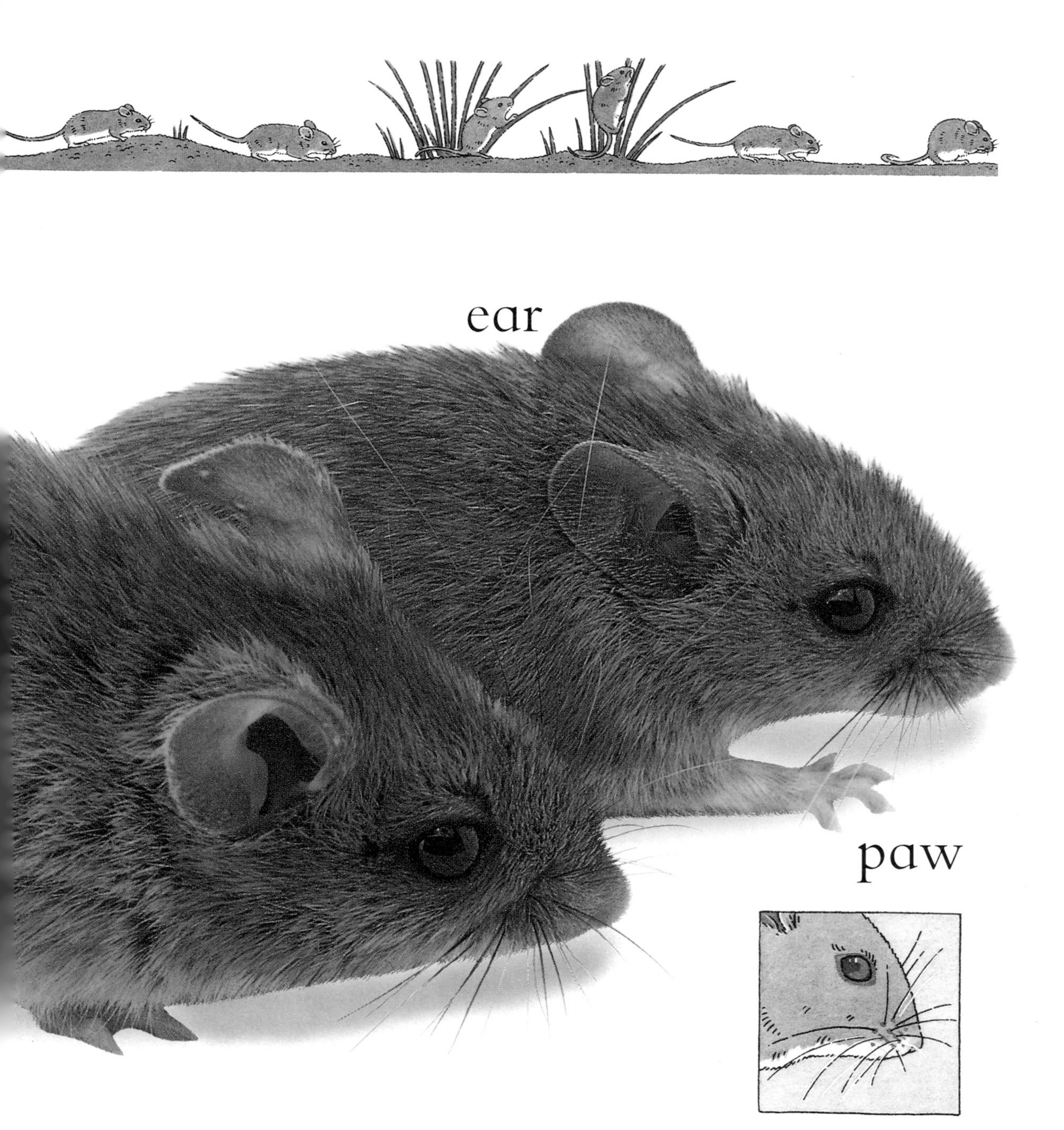

whiskers

Moth

wing

This moth lives
in the forest. During
the day it rests. The patterns
on its wings help the moth to
hide on tree bark. At night, the
moth flutters among the leaves,
looking for a place to lay its eggs.

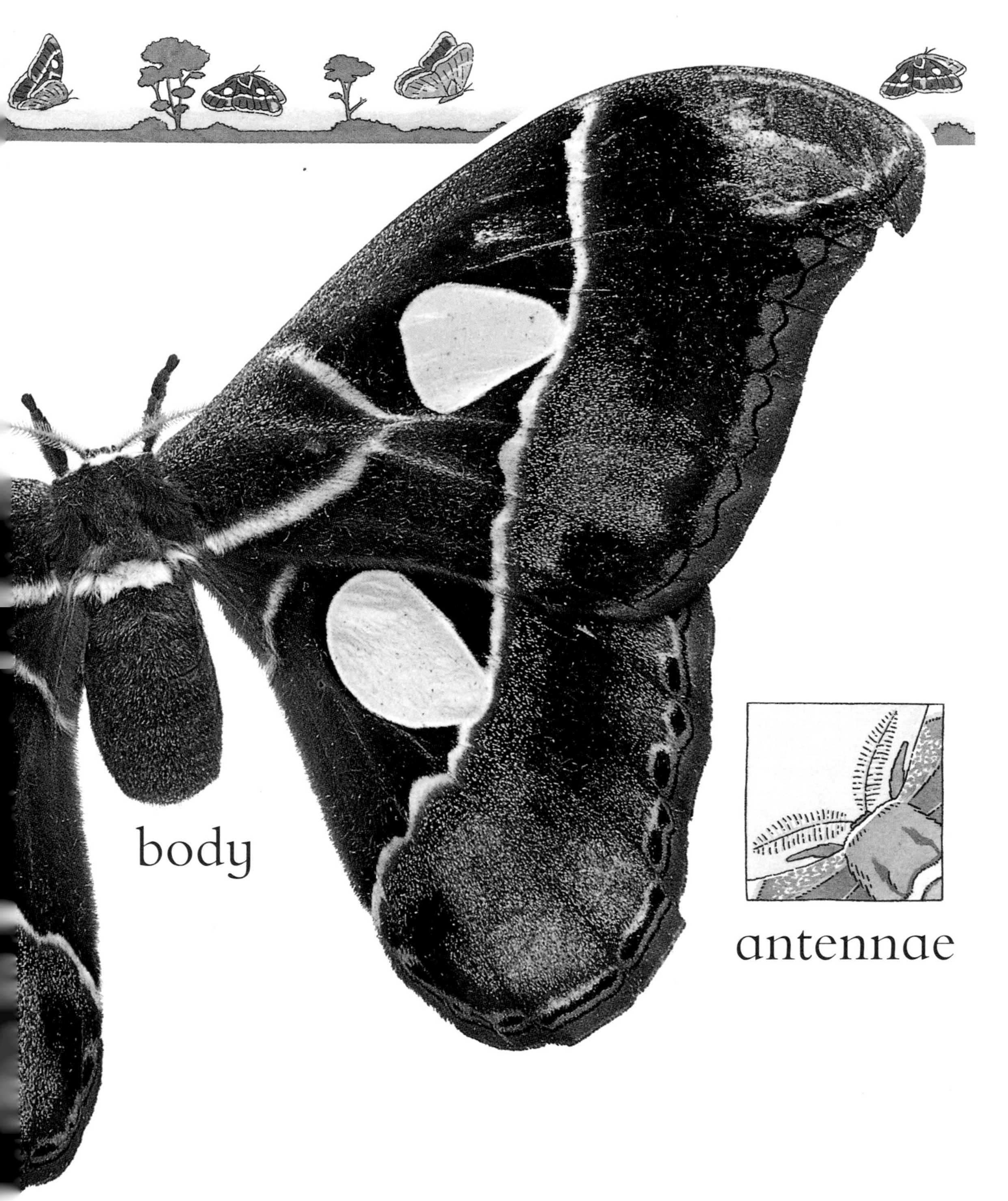
body
antennae

Panther

A panther is a black leopard. At night, it prowls through the forest hunting for food. The panther can smell when another animal passes nearby. During the day, the panther rests in the branches of a tree.

eye

head

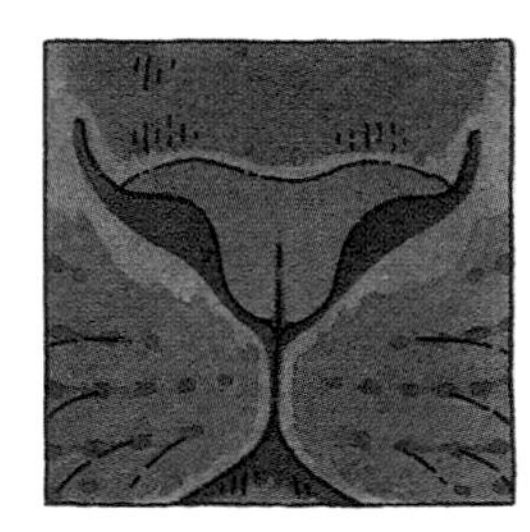

nose

paw

Scorpion

This scorpion lives in the desert. It hides in the sand during the day. At night, the scorpion catches insects in its claws. Then it stings them with the tip of its tail. Mother scorpions carry their babies on their backs.

claw

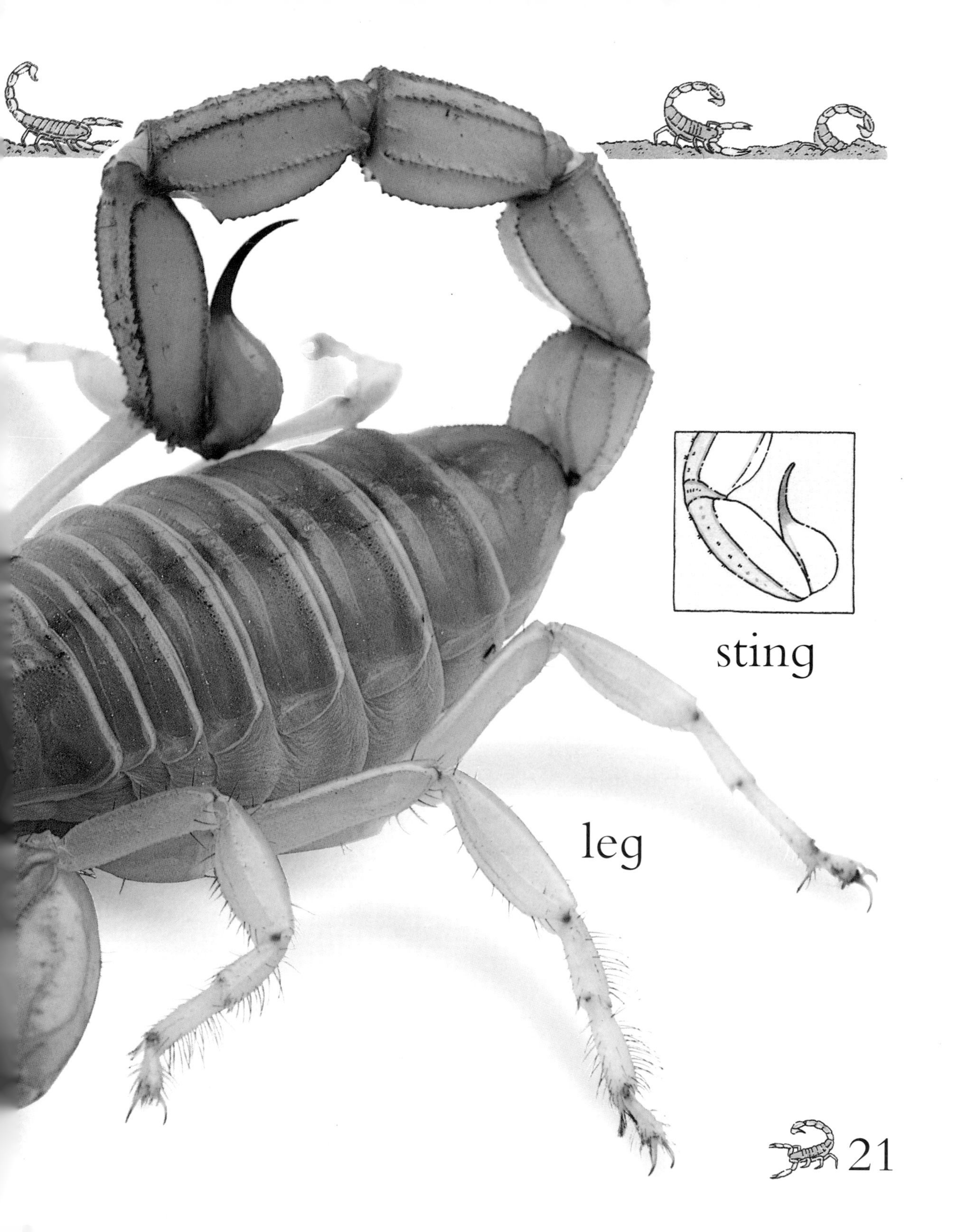
sting
leg